SOUPS

First edition for North America published in 2014
by Barron's Educational Series, Inc.

Copyright © McRae Publishing Ltd 2013 London

All inquiries should be addressed to:
Barron's Educational Series, Inc.
250 Wireless Boulevard
Hauppauge, New York 11788
www.barronseduc.com

Project Director Anne McRae
Art Director Marco Nardi
Photography Brent Parker Jones
Text Edith Bailey
Editing Dale Crawford, Daphne Trotter
Food Styling Lee Blaylock
Food Preparation Mark Hockenhull
Layouts Aurora Granata

ISBN: 978-1-4380-0418-1

Library of Congress Control Number: 2013943557

Printed in China
9 8 7 6 5 4 3 2 1

Scan and share The QR codes® in this book contain the ingredients list printed just above them. Easy and fun to use, they can be scanned by just about any smartphone or tablet, and the shopping list that pops up on your display can be forwarded and shared with a friend or partner at the supermarket, or just stored on your own device for use when shopping later in the day.

3 EASY STEPS: 1. Download onto your smartphone or tablet a "QR reader" (a simple App, often available for free); 2. Point the scanner at the QR code (the 3 black corner squares are key); 3. The shopping list pops up on your screen.

QR Codes® or Quick Response Codes are a type of barcode. They were invented in 1994 by and are a trademark of the Japanese firm Denso Wave, a subsidiary of Toyota, that granted their free use internationally. Granted patents are registered with the Patent Offices of Japan, the US, the UK and Europe.
The use of QR Codes is free of any license.
Granted QR Code patents: US 5726435 (in the USA), JP 2938338 (in Japan), EPO 0672994 (in the EU).

QR **WHAT YOU EAT**

SOUPS

Edith Bailey

BARRON'S

VEGETABLE stock

Makes
8 cups
(2 liters)

Preparation
10 min. + 30
min. to cool

Cooking
2 hr.

Level
Easy

2	tablespoons extra-virgin olive oil
2	large onions, coarsely chopped
1	turnip, peeled and coarsely chopped
2	carrots, peeled and coarsely chopped
4	stalks celery, coarsely chopped
	Salt
12	cups (3 liters) cold water + extra, to top up
	Small bunch fresh parsley
12	whole black peppercorns
3	dried bay leaves

Heat the oil in a large soup pot over medium-high heat. Add the onions, turnip, carrots, and celery, and sauté until lightly browned, about 5 minutes. Season with salt.

Add the water, parsley, peppercorns, and bay leaves and bring to a boil. Use a slotted spoon to remove any scum that rises to the surface. Reduce the heat to low and simmer, uncovered, for 2 hours, skimming the surface every 30 minutes or so. Top up with a little water from time to time.

Remove from the heat. Set aside to cool for 30 minutes.

Place a fine-mesh sieve over a large bowl. Carefully strain the stock into the bowl. Discard the solids in the sieve. Let cool to room temperature.

Cover the stock with plastic wrap (cling film) or place in an airtight container and store in the refrigerator. Use as directed in the recipes.

Homemade stock tastes so much better than stock made from stock or bouillon cubes. Making stock at home also allows you to control the amount of salt in the stock, which is ideal if you are following a low-sodium diet.

CHICKEN stock

Makes
3 quarts
(3 liters)

Preparation
10 min. + 30
min. to cool

Cooking
2 hr.

Level
Easy

1	(3-pound/1.5-kg) chicken
4	quarts (4 liters) cold water
1	onion, chopped
1	carrot, chopped
1	leek, chopped
2	bay leaves
2–3	sprigs fresh thyme
	Small bunch fresh parsley
8	black peppercorns
	Salt

Rinse the chicken thoroughly inside and out and place in a large soup pot with the water. Add the onion, carrot, leek, bay leaves, thyme, parsley, peppercorns, and salt.

Bring to a boil over medium heat. Use a slotted spoon to remove any scum that rises to the surface. Reduce the heat to low and simmer, uncovered, for 2 hours, skimming the surface every 30 minutes. Top up with a little water from time to time.

Remove from the heat. Set aside to cool for 30 minutes.

Place a fine-mesh sieve over a large bowl. Carefully strain the stock into the bowl. Discard the herbs and vegetables. Reserve the cooked chicken meat for use in salads, burgers, or pies. Let the stock cool completely, then chill overnight.

When ready to use, scoop the fat off the top with a large spoon and discard. Use as directed in the recipes.

Making stock at home is very easy but it does take some time to cook. The good thing is that you can make a large batch and either cover tightly and store in the refrigerator for several days, or freeze it for up to two months. When freezing, pour the stock into small containers (muffin pans are ideal) and freeze. Once solid, place the individual blocks of stock in a large plastic freezer bag and use as required.

BEEF stock

Makes
4 quarts
(4 liters)

Preparation
15 min. +
2½–3½ hr.
to cool

Cooking
4½ hr.

Level
Easy

3   pounds (1.5 kg) beef bones

2   onions, halved or quartered

2   carrots, coarsely chopped

2   stalks celery, coarsely chopped

    Small bunch fresh parsley

10   sprigs fresh thyme

2   bay leaves

5   quarts (5 liters) cold water

1   teaspoon whole black peppercorns

Preheat the oven to 400°F (200°C/gas 6). Place the beef bones, onions, carrots, and celery in a large roasting pan. Roast, stirring occasionally, for 1½ hours, until browned.

Tie the parsley, thyme, and bay leaves with kitchen string to make a bouquet garni.

Transfer the beef bones and vegetables into a large soup pot over medium-high heat. Scrape the brownings from the bottom of the roasting pan into the pot. Add the water, peppercorns, and bouquet garni. Bring to a boil, then reduce the heat to low. Simmer, uncovered, for 3 hours. Top up with a little water from time to time.

Remove from the heat. Set aside to cool for 30 minutes.

Place a fine-mesh sieve over a large bowl. Carefully strain the stock into the bowl. Discard the bouquet garni, vegetables, and beef bones. Let the stock cool completely, 2–3 hours.

Use as directed in the recipes.

This recipe makes a luscious stock, loaded with the delicious flavors of the roasted meat and vegetables.

GAZPACHO

Serves
6

Preparation
20 min. + 2-3
hr. to chill

Cooking
5 min.

Level
Easy

6	large slices, day-old, firm-textured bread, crusts removed
3	pounds (1.5 kg) ripe, fresh tomatoes
2	cucumbers, peeled, halved, and seeded
1	red bell pepper (capsicum), halved, seeded
1	red onion, halved
1	clove garlic
8	tablespoons (120 ml) extra-virgin olive oil + extra, to serve
1	tablespoon sherry vinegar
1	tablespoon freshly squeezed lemon juice
¼	teaspoon ground cumin
	Salt and freshly ground black pepper
2	stalks celery, with leaves attached
1	cup (120 g) blanched whole almonds, split

Cut three slices of the bread into small cubes and set aside. Soak the remaining three slices of bread in a bowl of water for 10 minutes. Squeeze out the excess water and set aside.

Cut a cross in the base of each tomato. Blanch in a pan of boiling water for 10 seconds. Let cool for a few minutes, then slip off the skins. Chop coarsely.

Coarsely chop one of the cucumbers, half the bell pepper, and half the onion, and add to the tomatoes.

Process the soaked bread and garlic in a food processor until a paste forms. Add the tomatoes and coarsely chopped vegetables and process until smooth.

With the motor running, gradually add 6 tablespoons (90 ml) of oil, the vinegar, lemon juice, and cumin. Season with salt and pepper. Chill for at least 2-3 hours, or until ready to serve.

When ready to serve, finely chop the celery, and the remaining cucumber, bell pepper, and onion, keeping them all separate.

Heat a small frying pan over medium heat. Add the almonds and cook, shaking the pan often, until golden. Set aside.

Heat the remaining oil in the same frying pan over medium heat. Add the bread cubes and cook, tossing until golden.

Serve the gazpacho chilled, drizzled with extra oil, and sprinkled with the chopped vegetables, fried bread, and almonds.

To garnish the gazpacho, just sprinkle a few of the vegetables, fried bread cubes, and almonds over each serving. Place the rest in small bowls on the table for people to help themselves.

CHILLED CUCUMBER SOUP

with garlic shrimp

Serves
4

Preparation
30 min. + 4
hr. to chill

Cooking
2-3 min.

Level
Easy

Soup

2½	large cucumbers, peeled
1¼	cups (300 ml) plain, thick Greek-style yogurt
⅓	cup (90 ml) crème fraîche
1¼	cups (300 ml) chicken stock (see page 6)
	Few drops Tabasco sauce
1	teaspoon salt
2	tablespoons chopped fresh mint
2	tablespoons chopped fresh chives
2	tablespoons chopped fresh dill

Garlic Shrimp

¼	cup (60 ml) extra-virgin olive oil
14	ounces (400 g) medium shrimp (prawns), peeled, tails on
4	cloves garlic, sliced
1	small red chili, seeded and thinly sliced
	Salt
1	cup (50 g) coarsely chopped fresh parsley
	Granary bread, to serve

Soup: Cut two of the cucumbers in half and scrape out the seeds. Coarsely chop the flesh and place in a food processor with the yogurt, crème fraîche, chicken stock, Tabasco, salt, mint, chives, and dill. Process until smooth.

Place in a bowl, cover, and chill for at least 4 hours.

Use a vegetable peeler to cut long strips from the remaining half cucumber. Cover and chill.

Garlic Shrimp: Heat the oil in a medium frying pan over medium-high heat. Add the shrimp, garlic, and chili and sauté until the shrimp are cooked through, 2-3 minutes. Season with salt. Add the parsley and toss gently. Let cool to room temperature.

Ladle the soup into four soup bowls. Place a pile of the garlic shrimp mixture in the center of each bowl. Garnish with the chilled cucumber strips, and serve with the granary bread.

Serve this elegant soup for lunch during the hot summer months.

CREAM OF SPINACH soup

Serves
4–6

Preparation
15 min. + 10 min. to cool

Cooking
20–25 min.

Level
Easy

2	tablespoons extra-virgin olive oil
1	onion, coarsely chopped
2	cloves garlic, finely chopped
2	teaspoons ground cumin
5	cups (1.25 liters) vegetable or chicken stock (see pages 4 or 6)
2	pounds (1 kg) potatoes, peeled and coarsely chopped
4	cups (200 g) spinach
	Salt and freshly ground black pepper
¼	cup (60 ml) sour cream
	Crusty bread, to serve

Heat the oil in a large soup pot over medium heat. Add the onion, garlic, and cumin and sauté until softened, 3–4 minutes.

Increase the heat to high. Add the vegetable or chicken stock and bring to a boil. Add the potatoes, then decrease the heat to medium-low. Simmer, uncovered, until the potatoes are tender, about 10 minutes. Add the spinach and cook until wilted, 2–3 minutes. Set aside for 10 minutes to cool.

Purée the soup with a handheld blender until smooth. Return to medium-low heat and simmer, stirring constantly, until heated through, 4–5 minutes. Remove from the heat. Season with salt and pepper.

Ladle the soup into four to six serving bowls. Top with a dollop of sour cream and season with pepper. Serve hot with plenty of crusty bread.

Spinach is packed with vitamins, minerals, and antioxidants. Low in calories and fat, it should be part of every healthy diet. In our recipe, we have teamed it with potatoes, to add energy-giving carbs.

BELL PEPPER SOUP

with spicy cornbread

Serves
4–6

Preparation
30 min.

Cooking
30–40 min.

Level
Medium

Soup

1	tablespoon extra-virgin olive oil
2	red onions, chopped
2	cloves garlic, chopped
3	pounds (1.5 kg) red bell peppers (capsicums), seeded and chopped
1	(14-ounce/400-g) can diced tomatoes, with juice
6	cups (1.5 liters) chicken stock (see page 6)
1	cup (250 ml) heavy (double) cream
	Salt and freshly ground black pepper
¼	cup finely chopped fresh chives

Cornbread

1	cup (170 g) cornmeal
1	cup (150 g) all-purpose (plain) flour
1	teaspoon baking powder
¼	teaspoon salt
1	cup (250 ml) milk
⅓	cup (90 g) butter, melted
1	large egg, lightly beaten
1	teaspoon hot chili powder
1	cup (120 g) coarsely grated Cheddar cheese

Soup: Heat the oil in a soup pot over medium heat. Add the onions and garlic and sauté until softened, 3–4 minutes. Add the bell peppers and sauté for 5 minutes.

Add the tomatoes and chicken stock and bring to a boil. Decrease the heat and simmer, uncovered, stirring occasionally, until the bell peppers are tender, about 20 minutes.

Remove from the heat and purée with a handheld blender. Add the cream and stir over low heat until hot. Season with salt and pepper.

Cornbread: Preheat the oven to 350°F (180°C/gas 4). Lightly grease 8–12 muffin cups.

Combine the cornmeal, flour, baking powder, and salt in a large bowl. Add the milk, butter, egg, and chili powder, and stir until well combined. Stir in the cheese.

Spoon the mixture into the prepared muffin pan. Bake for 20–25 minutes, until a toothpick inserted into the center comes out clean. Turn onto a wire rack to cool slightly.

Ladle the soup into serving bowls. Sprinkle with the chives, and serve hot with the warm cornbread.

Get the soup underway, then prepare the cornbread and pop it in the oven while the soup finishes cooking.

BUTTERNUT SQUASH soup

Serves
4–6

Preparation
20 min.

Cooking
25–30 min.

Level
Easy

2 tablespoons butter

1 small onion, chopped

1 (2-inch/5-cm) piece fresh ginger, peeled and finely chopped

2 cloves garlic, chopped

3 pounds (1.5 kg) small butternut squash, peeled, seeds removed, and cut into small cubes

4 cups (1 liter) cold water

¼ cup (60 ml) freshly squeezed orange juice

Salt and freshly ground black pepper

Sour cream, to serve

Cilantro (coriander), to serve

Melt the butter in a large soup pot over medium heat. Add the onion and sauté until softened, 3–4 minutes.

Stir in the ginger, garlic, and squash and cook, stirring often, until beginning to soften, 6–8 minutes. Stir in the water. Bring to a boil, then decrease the heat to low and simmer until the squash is tender, 15–20 minutes.

Remove from the heat and purée with a handheld blender. Stir in the orange juice and season with salt and pepper. Serve hot, garnished with sour cream, extra pepper, and cilantro.

Butternut squash, also known as butternut pumpkin, has a deep orange color and a rich flavor. This versatile vegetable is an excellent source of vitamins A and E. It is also rich in dietary fiber, vitamin C, potassium, and manganese.

MINTY PEA & PANCETTA soup

Serves
4

Preparation
15 min.

Cooking
20 min.

Level
Easy

5   ounces (150 g) of cubed pancetta

2   medium potatoes, peeled and chopped

4   cups (1 liter) chicken stock (see page 6)

4   cups (600 g) frozen peas

Small bunch fresh mint, chopped

Garlic bread, to serve

Dry-fry the pancetta in a soup pot over medium heat until crisp and golden brown, 4–5 minutes. Scoop out about one-third of the pancetta and set aside as a garnish.

Add the potatoes and chicken stock to the pot and simmer until the potatoes are tender, about 10 minutes. Add the peas and simmer for 5 minutes. Stir in the mint.

Remove from the heat and purée with a handheld blender.

Ladle into four serving bowls. Garnish with the reserved pancetta, and serve hot with the garlic bread.

Green peas are low in fat and cholesterol and a good source of lean plant protein, dietary fiber, and vitamins A, C, K, and thiamine. Serve this hearty soup in the winter months as an appetizer or lunch.

HOT & SPICY tomato & bean soup

Serves
4

Preparation
15 min.

Cooking
18–20 min.

Level
Easy

4   cloves garlic, chopped

3   dried hot red chiles, crumbled + extra, to serve

1   teaspoon coriander

¾   teaspoon coarse salt

⅛   teaspoon caraway seeds

2   tablespoons extra-virgin olive oil

1   (14-ounce/400-g) can garbanzo beans (chickpeas), drained and rinsed

1   (14-ounce/400-g) can tomatoes, with juice

4   cups (1 liter) chicken stock (see page 6)

Fresh basil, to garnish

Sour cream, to serve

Crush the garlic, chilies, coriander, salt, and caraway seeds with a pestle and mortar or spice grinder to form a paste.

Heat the oil in a soup pot over medium heat. Add the garlic mixture, and sauté until fragrant, 1–2 minutes.

Stir in the garbanzo beans, tomatoes, and chicken stock. Bring to a boil, then simmer, stirring often, for 15 minutes. Let cool slightly.

Remove the pot from the heat and purée with a handheld blender.

Return to medium-low heat and stir until warmed through. Ladle into four serving bowls. Garnish with the basil and sour cream and serve hot, with extra chilies in a small bowl passed separately so everyone can help themselves.

Use more or less chili, according to taste. If not all your guests like spicy food, just add one chili to the soup and pass the rest separately.

SWEET POTATO & CARROT

soup

Serves
4

Preparation
20 min.

Cooking
20–25 min.

Level
Easy

2	tablespoons extra-virgin olive oil
1	large onion, coarsely chopped
2	cloves garlic, finely chopped
2	teaspoons finely grated fresh ginger
2	teaspoons ground cumin
1	pound (500 g) sweet potatoes, peeled and coarsely chopped
1	pound (500 g) carrots, peeled and coarsely chopped
4	cups (1 liter) vegetable or chicken stock (see pages 4 or 6)
	Salt and freshly ground black pepper
½	cup (120 ml) plain, low-fat yogurt
	Chopped fresh chives, to serve

Heat the oil in a large soup pot over medium heat. Add the onion and sauté until softened, 3–4 minutes. Add the garlic, ginger, and cumin. Sauté until aromatic, 1–2 minutes.

Add the sweet potatoes, carrots, and vegetable or chicken stock. Increase the heat to high and bring to a boil. Cover and reduce the heat to low. Simmer until the vegetables are soft, 15–20 minutes.

Remove from the heat and purée with a handheld blender. Return the soup to low heat and stir until heated through. Season with salt and pepper.

Ladle the soup into four serving bowls. Top each bowl with a dollop of yogurt and some chives, and serve hot.

Bursting with flavor and goodness, you can serve this soup on any occasion throughout the year.

CREAM OF MUSHROOM soup

Serves
4

Preparation
20 min. + 15
min. to soak

Cooking
30–35 min.

Level
Easy

1   ounce (30 g) dried porcini
    (ceps) mushrooms

4   tablespoons (60 g) butter

1   onion, finely chopped

2   cloves garlic, sliced

1   tablespoon fresh thyme
    + extra sprigs, to serve

1   pound (500 g) mixed wild
    mushrooms

4   cups (1 liter) vegetable
    stock (see page 4)

1   cup (250 ml) light crème
    fraîche or thick, plain,
    Greek-style yogurt

4   slices firm-textured bread,
    cubed

Put the dried porcini in a bowl and cover with boiling water. Let soak for 15 minutes.

Heat 2 tablespoons of butter in a soup pot over medium heat. Add the onion, garlic, and thyme and sauté until softened and starting to brown, 4–5 minutes.

Drain the porcini, reserving the soaking liquid, and add to the onion along with the mixed wild mushrooms. Let simmer until the mushrooms soften, about 5 minutes.

Pour in the vegetable stock and the soaking liquid, bring to a boil, then simmer for 20 minutes. Stir in the crème fraîche, and simmer for a few minutes more.

Remove from the heat and purée with a handheld blender.

Heat the remaining 2 tablespoons of butter in a large frying pan over medium heat and fry the bread cubes until crisp and golden brown.

Return the soup to the heat and warm over medium-low heat. Ladle into four serving bowls, sprinkle with the fried bread and extra thyme, and serve hot.

If you are lucky enough to live in an area where porcini mushrooms grow in abundance—and are in season—then replace the mixed wild mushrooms in this recipe with the same quantity of porcini and eliminate the dried porcini.

CAULIFLOWER SOUP with hot scones

Serves
6

Preparation
20 min.

Cooking
30–40 min.

Level
Medium

Soup

2	tablespoons extra-virgin olive oil + extra, to serve
1	large onion, chopped
2	cloves garlic, chopped
3	pounds (1.5 kg) cauliflower, cut into florets
1	pound (500 g) potatoes, peeled and chopped
4	cups (1 liter) chicken stock (see page 6)
	Freshly ground black pepper
½	cup (120 ml) heavy (double) cream
	Ground cumin, to dust
	Fresh sage leaves, to garnish

Scones

1	cup (150 g) self-raising flour
½	teaspoon salt
½	teaspoon ground cumin
2	tablespoons butter
½	cup (120 ml) milk + extra, to brush
4	ounces (120 g) blue cheese, finely chopped

Soup: Heat the oil in a large saucepan over medium heat. Add the onion and garlic and sauté until softened, 3–4 minutes. Add the cauliflower and potatoes and sauté for 5 minutes.

Add the chicken stock. Season with pepper. Cover and bring to a boil. Decrease the heat to low and simmer until the potatoes are tender, 15–20 minutes.

Remove from the heat and purée with a handheld blender.

Scones: Preheat the oven to 350°F (180°C/gas 4). Line a baking sheet with parchment paper.

Sift the flour, salt, and cumin into a bowl. Use your fingertips to rub the butter into the flour mixture until it resembles fine bread crumbs. Add the milk and cheese and mix until combined. Turn out onto a floured work surface and knead gently until smooth.

Roll out the dough to about ¾ inch (2 cm) thick. Cut into 10–12 scones. Place the scones on the prepared baking sheet. Brush the tops with extra milk.

Bake for 15 minutes, until golden brown. Wrap the hot scones loosely in a clean kitchen towel to keep warm.

Return the soup to low heat. Add the cream and simmer, stirring, until heated through, 2–3 minutes. Ladle into bowls, dust with cumin, garnish with sage leaves, and drizzle with extra oil. Serve hot with the warm scones.

This soup and scone combo makes a wonderful lunch. You will need a large head of cauliflower, weighing about 3 pounds (1.5 kg). If preferred, replace the cauliflower with the same weight of broccoli.

CREAMY TOMATO SOUP

with pesto

Serves
6

Preparation
15 min.

Cooking
15–20 min.

Level
Easy

2	tablespoons extra-virgin olive oil
2	cloves garlic, chopped
5	sun-dried tomatoes in oil, drained and coarsely chopped
3	(14-ounce/400-g) cans tomatoes, with juice
2	cups (500 ml) vegetable stock (see page 4)
1	teaspoon sugar
	Salt and freshly ground black pepper
²⁄₃	cup (150 ml) sour cream
½	cup (120 ml) storebought or homemade basil pesto (see recipe below)
	Fresh basil leaves, to serve
	Grissini (bead sticks), to serve

Heat the oil in a soup pot over medium-low heat. Add the garlic and sauté until softened, 3–4 minutes. Add the sun-dried tomatoes, canned tomatoes, vegetable stock, sugar, salt, and pepper. Bring to a boil, then simmer over low heat until the tomatoes have broken down a little, 10–15 minutes.

Remove from the heat and purée with a handheld blender, adding the sour cream.

Return the soup to low heat and simmer, stirring, until heated through, 2–3 minutes. Ladle into bowls, and garnish with a dollop of pesto and some fresh basil leaves. Serve hot with the grissini.

Basil and tomato are a classic flavor combination and they work especially well in this soup. You can buy good-quality fresh pesto in Italian delis and supermarkets, but if you prefer, it is easy to make at home. Just chop a large bunch of fresh basil with 2 cloves of garlic, 2 tablespoons each of pine nuts and Parmesan cheese, and ½ cup (120 ml) of extra-virgin olive oil in a food processor until smooth. Season with salt and pepper and serve.

BORSCHT

Serves
4–6

Preparation
20 min.

Cooking
2 hr.

Level
Easy

1	pound (500 g) beets (beetroot/red beet), peeled and quartered
1	carrot, peeled and chopped
1	parsnip, peeled and cut into chunks
1	leek, white part only, sliced
1	onion, chopped
⅓	cup (90 ml) freshly squeezed lemon juice
½	teaspoon allspice
½	teaspoon nutmeg
3	bay leaves
6	cups (1.5 liters) beef stock (see page 8)
	Salt and freshly ground black pepper
1	cup (250 ml) sour cream
4	tablespoons chopped fresh dill
	Rye bread, to serve

Put the beets, carrot, parsnip, leek, onion, lemon juice, allspice, nutmeg, and bay leaves in a soup pot with the beef stock. Bring to a boil, then decrease the heat to low and simmer, partially covered, for 2 hours.

Remove from the heat and purée with a handheld blender. Season with salt and pepper.

Return the soup to low heat and simmer, stirring, until heated through, 2–3 minutes. Ladle into bowls and garnish with the sour cream and dill. Serve hot with the rye bread.

Borscht originally comes from the Ukraine, but it is popular in many eastern and central European countries. There are several variations on the recipe, but beets are the key ingredient, giving the soup its characteristic color and flavor.

TOMATO & BACON SOUP

with garlic croutons

Serves
4–6

Preparation
20 min.

Cooking
30–35 min.

Level
Easy

Soup

2 tablespoons extra-virgin olive oil

3½ ounces (100 g) bacon, finely chopped

1 onion, finely chopped

3 stalks celery, finely chopped

2 carrots, finely chopped

2 cloves garlic, finely chopped

½ teaspoon red pepper flakes

2 (14-ounce/400-g) cans tomatoes, with juice

2 cups (500 ml) water

Croutons

4 cloves garlic, finely chopped

¼ cup (60 ml) extra-virgin olive oil

3 large thick slices granary bread, cut into cubes

Fresh basil, to serve

Soup: Heat the oil in a large soup pot over medium heat. Add the bacon, onion, celery, and carrots and sauté until softened, about 5 minutes. Add the garlic and red pepper flakes and sauté until aromatic, about 1 minute.

Add the tomatoes and water. Bring to a boil then decrease the heat to low. Simmer, stirring occasionally, for about 25 minutes.

Croutons: While the soup is simmering, preheat the oven to 400°F (200°C/gas 6). Combine the garlic and oil in a bowl. Add the cubes of bread and toss to coat. Place on a baking sheet and bake for 10 minutes, until crisp and golden brown.

Remove the soup from the heat and purée with a handheld blender.

Return the soup to low heat and simmer, stirring, until heated through, 2–3 minutes. Ladle into serving bowls. Serve hot, garnished with the croutons and basil.

Make sure that the croutons are well coated in the garlic and oil. They should become crisp and golden brown in the oven.

BROCCOLI SOUP

with herb scones

Serves
6

Preparation
20 min.

Cooking
20–25 min.

Level
Easy

Soup

2	tablespoons extra-virgin olive oil
2	tablespoons butter
2	pounds (1 kg) broccoli, broken into florets, stems chopped
1	clove garlic, finely chopped
5	cups (1.25 liters) vegetable or chicken stock (see page 4 or 6)
	Salt and freshly ground black pepper
	Fresh chives, snipped, to garnish

Scones

1½	cups (225 g) all-purpose (plain) flour
1½	teaspoons baking powder
2	tablespoons butter
1	tablespoon finely chopped fresh chives
2	teaspoons finely chopped fresh oregano
¾	cup (180 ml) milk

Soup: Heat the oil and butter in a soup pot over medium heat. Add the broccoli stems and garlic, and sauté until tender, 3–4 minutes. Stir in the florets.

Add the stock and bring to a boil. Cover the pot and simmer over low heat until the broccoli is tender, about 10 minutes.

Scones: Preheat the oven to 450°F (230°C/gas 8). Line a baking sheet with parchment paper.

Combine the flour, baking powder, and butter in a bowl. Rub in the butter until the mixture resembles fine bread crumbs. Add the chives and oregano and season with salt and pepper.

Make a well in the center. Add the milk and mix until a soft but sticky dough forms. Turn out onto a lightly floured work surface and pat into a ¾-inch (2-cm) thick disk. Score into 10–12 scones (cut about halfway through the dough).

Place on the prepared baking sheet. Bake for 10 minutes, until golden brown. Wrap the hot scones loosely in a clean kitchen towel to keep warm.

When the broccoli is tender, remove the soup from the heat and purée with a handheld blender.

Return the soup to low heat and simmer, stirring, until heated through, 2–3 minutes. Season with salt and pepper. Ladle into serving bowls and garnish with the chives. Serve hot with the scones.

FRENCH ONION soup

Serves
6

Preparation
25 min.

Cooking
1½ hr.

Level
Medium

¼ cup (60 g) butter

2 pounds (1 kg) yellow onions, peeled, halved, and thinly sliced

1 teaspoon sugar

1 tablespoon all-purpose (plain) flour

½ cup (120 ml) dry sherry

4 cups (1 liter) beef stock (see page 8)

2 teaspoons finely chopped fresh thyme

Salt and freshly ground black pepper

1 small baguette (French loaf), sliced

2 cups (200 g) Gruyère cheese, coarsely grated

Melt the butter in a large soup pot over very low heat. Add the onions. Sprinkle with the sugar, and cook, stirring often, until caramelized, about 1 hour.

Sprinkle the flour over the onions, stirring to coat. Add the sherry, beef stock, and thyme, and bring to a boil. Partially cover the pot and simmer gently for 30 minutes. Season with salt and pepper.

Meanwhile, preheat an overhead broiler (grill) and lightly toast the bread.

Ladle the soup into six ovenproof serving bowls. Arrange the bowls in a baking pan. Place 2–3 slices of toasted bread in each bowl. Sprinkle with the grated cheese, and place under the broiler until the cheese is melted and crusty brown around the edges, 3–5 minutes. Serve hot.

This onion soup is a classic, both in France and abroad. There are many variations, but the modern recipe is usually based on slowly caramelized onions, simmered with beef stock, and topped with a broiled (grilled) bread and cheese topping.

BARLEY & VEGGIE soup

Serves
4

Preparation
20 min.

Cooking
50–55 min.

Level
Easy

2	tablespoons extra-virgin olive oil
1	onion, chopped
1	carrot, chopped
4	slices bacon, rinds removed and chopped
2	stalks celery, leaves reserved, stalks chopped
1	(14-ounce/400-g) can tomatoes, with juice
1	large zucchini (courgette), chopped
6	cups (1.5 liters) chicken stock (see page 6)
½	cup (100 g) pearl barley

Heat the oil in a soup pan over medium heat. Add the onion, carrot, bacon, and celery stalks and sauté until softened, 5–7 minutes.

Add the tomatoes, zucchini, chicken stock, and barley and bring to a boil. Reduce the heat, partially covered, and simmer over low heat until the barley is tender, about 45 minutes.

Chop the reserved celery leaves. Stir into the soup. Ladle into serving bowls, and serve hot.

Serve this light and nourishing soup with grissini (bread sticks) or freshly baked, crusty bread.

CORN chowder

Serves
4

Preparation
15 min.

Cooking
7–10 min.

Level
Easy

2	tablespoons extra-virgin olive oil
1	small onion, finely chopped
4	cups (1 liter) vegetable stock (see page 4)
2	cups (500 ml) water
1	(14-ounce/400-g) can creamed corn
1	(14-ounce/400-g) can corn (sweetcorn), drained
4	shallots, thinly sliced
	Fresh cilantro (coriander), to serve

Heat the oil in a soup pot over medium heat. Add the onion and sauté until softened, 3–4 minutes.

Add the vegetable stock, water, creamed corn, and corn and bring to a boil.

Reduce the heat to medium. Stir in about three-quarters of the shallots and simmer for 4–6 minutes. Season with salt and pepper.

Ladle the chowder into serving bowls. Top with the remaining shallots and the cilantro, and serve hot.

Traditionally, a chowder is a very thick soup, made with corn, clams, or fish, but there are many modern variations.

MOROCCAN TOMATO & BEAN soup

Serves
4

Preparation
15 min.

Cooking
40 min.

Level
Easy

2 tablespoons extra-virgin olive oil

1 large onion, chopped

2 carrots, diced

3 stalks celery, diced

2–3 tablespoons harissa paste

1 teaspoon ground cumin

1 (14-ounce/400-g) can tomatoes, with juice

2 tablespoons tomato purée

3 cups (750 ml) vegetable stock (see page 4)

1 (14-ounce/400-g) garbanzo beans (chickpeas), drained and rinsed

4 tablespoons couscous

3 tablespoons coarsely chopped fresh parsley

Heat the oil in a soup pot over medium heat. Add the onion, carrots, and celery and sauté until softened, about 5 minutes. Add the harissa paste and cumin, stirring well.

Stir in the tomatoes, tomato purée, vegetable stock, and garbanzo beans and stir well. Cover and simmer for 30 minutes. Add the couscous and simmer for 5 minutes.

Stir in the parsley. Ladle into serving bowls, and serve hot.

Serve this soup with warm focaccia or flatbread, or thicken it even more with extra couscous.

EASY THAI SHRIMP & COCONUT soup

Serves
4

Preparation
15 min.

Cooking
10 min.

Level
Easy

2	tablespoons Thai red curry paste
1	(14-ounce/400-ml) can coconut milk
8	ounces (250 g) fresh corn (sweetcorn), sliced off the ears (cobs)
16	cherry tomatoes, halved
1	red chili, seeded and thinly sliced
8	ounces (250 g) raw shrimp (prawns), heads removed and peeled
2	cups (500 ml) boiling chicken stock (see page 6)
4	tablespoons coarsely chopped fresh cilantro (coriander)

Heat the red curry paste in a soup pot over medium heat until it starts to sizzle in its own oil. Stir in the coconut milk and bring to a gentle simmer.

Add the corn and simmer for 3–4 minutes. Add the cherry tomatoes, chili, and shrimp and simmer for 3–4 minutes more. Add the chicken stock and stir in the cilantro.

Ladle into four serving bowls, and serve hot.

Thai curry paste can be bought in the Asian section of supermarkets and from Asian food stores.

CHICKEN chowder

Serves
8

Preparation
30 min.

Cooking
1½ hr.

Level
Medium

1	whole chicken (about 4 pounds/2 kg)
8	cups (2 liters) water
1	large onion, ½ left whole, ½ chopped
2	carrots, 1 halved lengthwise, 1 cut into ½-inch (1-cm) dice
4	stems fresh parsley
10	whole black peppercorns
2	tablespoons butter
2	tablespoons all-purpose (plain) flour
1	small turnip, cut into ½-inch (1-cm) cubes
1	parsnip, cut into ½-inch (1-cm) cubes
	Salt
½	cup (120 ml) heavy (double) cream
	Freshly ground black pepper
1	tablespoon chopped fresh dill, to garnish

Put the chicken in a large soup pot. Add the water, onion half, carrot halves, parsley, and peppercorns. Bring to a boil, then decrease the heat to low, partially cover, and simmer gently for 1 hour.

Remove the chicken and let cool. Strain the stock through a fine-mesh sieve into another pot, and bring to a simmer. Simmer for 20 minutes to reduce and intensify the flavor.

Shred the chicken into bite-size pieces, discarding the skin and bones.

Melt the butter in a large soup pot over medium heat. Add the chopped onion and diced carrot, and sauté until softened, about 5 minutes.

Stir in the flour, and cook, stirring constantly, for 1 minute. Whisk in the chicken stock, and bring to a boil. Add the turnip, parsnip, and 1 teaspoon of salt. Decrease the heat to low, and simmer until the turnip and parsnip are tender, about 10 minutes.

Stir in the chicken meat and cream. Heat until warmed through, 2–3 minutes. Season with pepper, and garnish with the dill. Ladle into soup bowls, and serve hot.

This is a hearty and nourishing soup that can be served as a complete meal.

CHICKEN laksa

Serves
4

Preparation
15 min.

Cooking
10–15 min.

Level
Easy

2 tablespoons laksa paste

4 cups (1 liter) chicken stock (see page 6)

1 (14-ounce/400-ml) can coconut milk

2 boneless, skinless chicken breasts, thinly sliced

8 ounces (250 g) vermicelli noodles

1 tablespoon freshly squeezed lime juice

1 tablespoon Thai fish sauce

1 teaspoon brown sugar

1 cup (50 g) fresh bean sprouts, to serve

Scallions (spring onions), thinly sliced, to serve

Fresh cilantro (coriander), to serve

Place a soup pot over medium heat. Add the laksa paste and stir until fragrant, about 1 minute. Stir in the chicken stock and coconut milk.

Bring to a simmer, add the chicken, and simmer until just cooked through, about 5 minutes.

While the chicken is cooking, place the noodles in a large heatproof bowl and cover with boiling water. Let soak until softened, 3–4 minutes. Drain and set aside.

Stir the lime juice, fish sauce, and brown sugar into the laksa mixture.

To serve, divide the noodles evenly among four large soup bowls. Ladle in the chicken laksa mixture and top with bean sprouts, scallions, and cilantro. Serve immediately.

Laksa soup is a spicy noodle soup often served in the Southeast Asian countries of Malaysia, Singapore, and Indonesia. There are two main types of laksa: a sweet and spicy coconut and noodle soup (like ours), and a sour fish and noodle soup. Laksa paste can be bought in the Asian section of supermarkets and from Asian food stores.

AZTEC CHICKEN soup

Serves
4

Preparation
20 min.

Cooking
25–30 min.

Level
Easy

2	boneless, skinless chicken breasts
1	chicken stock cube
4	cups (1 liter) water
2	tablespoons extra-virgin olive oil
1	red onion, finely chopped
1	tablespoon ground cumin
1	teaspoon chili powder
1	(14-ounce/400-g) can tomatoes, with juice
1	(14-ounce/400-g) can red kidney beans, drained and rinsed
	Salt and freshly ground black pepper
1	large avocado, halved, peeled, coarsely chopped
1	(14-ounce/400-g) can corn (sweetcorn) kernels, drained
½	cup coarsely chopped fresh cilantro (coriander)
1	tablespoon freshly squeezed lime juice
	Spicy (paprika) corn chips, to serve

Put the chicken and stock cube in a saucepan and cover with the water. Bring to a boil, then decrease the heat to low. Simmer until the chicken is cooked through, 8–10 minutes. Use tongs to transfer the chicken to a plate. Reserve the cooking liquid. Let the chicken cool slightly, then shred.

Heat the oil in a soup pot over medium heat. Add the onion and sauté until softened, 3–4 minutes. Add the cumin and chili, and stir for 30 seconds, until aromatic. Add the reserved cooking liquid and tomatoes and bring to a boil.

Add the shredded chicken and kidney beans and return to a boil. Decrease the heat to medium-low and simmer, stirring occasionally, until the soup thickens, about 10 minutes. Season with salt and pepper.

While the soup is cooking, combine the avocado, corn, cilantro, and lime juice in a small bowl.

Ladle the soup into serving bowls. Top with spoonfuls of the avocado mixture, and serve hot with the corn chips.

Avocado, lime, cilantro, beans, chili, and corn chips—the flavors of Mexico! This warming soup makes a delicious lunch.

MEATBALL soup

Serves
6

Preparation
20 min.

Cooking
15–20 min.

Level
Medium

1	pound (500 g) lean ground (minced) pork
2	cloves garlic, finely chopped
1	small onion, finely chopped
4	tablespoons finely chopped fresh parsley
½	teaspoon red pepper flakes
1	cup (150 g) fine dry bread crumbs
½	cup (60 g) freshly grated Parmesan cheese + extra, to serve
	Salt and freshly ground black pepper
2	tablespoons extra-virgin olive oil
6	cups (1.5 liters) chicken stock (see page 6)
3½	ounces (100 g) angel-hair pasta, broken into short pieces

Combine the pork, garlic, onion, 2 tablespoons of parsley, the red pepper flakes, bread crumbs, and Parmesan in a bowl. Season with salt and pepper. Mix well, then shape into small meatballs.

Heat the oil in a large frying pan over medium-low heat. Fry the meatballs until golden brown, 8–10 minutes. Let drain on paper towels.

Add the chicken stock to the same pan and bring to a boil. Add the pasta and cook for 1 minute. Add the meatballs and simmer gently over low heat until the pasta is cooked al dente, 2–3 minutes.

Ladle the soup into serving bowls and garnish with the remaining 2 tablespoons of parsley and the extra Parmesan. Serve hot.

54

LAMB & BARLEY soup

Serves
6

Preparation
20 min.

Cooking
45–55 min.

Level
Easy

2   tablespoons extra-virgin olive oil

12 ounces (350 g) lamb neck fillet, trimmed, and cut into small pieces

Salt and freshly ground black pepper

2   small onions, finely chopped

1   cup (200 g) pearl barley

1½ pounds (750 g) mixed root vegetables, such as potatoes, carrots, sweet potatoes, turnip, cubed

1   tablespoon Worcestershire sauce

6   cups (1.5 liters) beef stock (see page 8)

1   sprig fresh thyme + extra, to garnish

5   ounces (150 g) green beans, trimmed and cut into short lengths

Thick slices of granary bread, to serve

Heat the oil in a soup pot over medium heat. Season the lamb with salt and pepper. Add to the pot and sauté until browned all over, about 5 minutes.

Add the onions and barley, and sauté until the onions are softened, 3–4 minutes. Add the root vegetables and sauté for 2 more minutes. Add the Worcestershire sauce, beef stock, and thyme. Partially cover the pot and simmer until the meat is tender, 35–45 minutes.

Add the green beans about 10 minutes before the meat is ready.

Ladle the soup into bowls, garnish with thyme, and serve hot with the bread.

Somewhere between a stew and a soup, this hearty dish makes a meal in itself and is perfect for cold winter days.

LENTIL & BACON soup

Serves
4

Preparation
15 min.

Cooking
30–40 min.

Level
Easy

2   tablespoons extra-virgin olive oil

1   onion, finely chopped

5   ounces (150 g) pancetta, cut into small cubes

1   carrot, cut into small cubes

1   teaspoon ground cumin

½   teaspoon ground turmeric

2   cloves garlic, finely chopped

1   chili, seeded and finely chopped

6   cups (1.5 liters) chicken stock (see page 6)

1½   cups (250 g) red lentils

1   tablespoon coarsely chopped fresh parsley, to serve

Heat the oil in a soup pot over low heat. Add the onion, half the pancetta, and the carrot. Simmer until the vegetables are softened, 7–10 minutes.

Add the cumin, turmeric, garlic, and chili and cook until aromatic, 2–3 minutes.

Pour in the chicken stock and add the lentils. Bring to a boil, then cover, and simmer over low heat, stirring occasionally, until the lentils are tender, 20–25 minutes.

Just before the soup is ready, dry-fry the remaining pancetta in a small frying pan over medium heat until crisp and golden.

Ladle the soup into serving bowls, sprinkle with the fried pancetta and the parsley, and serve hot.

Lentils are a good source of lean protein, as well as dietary fiber, vitamin B1, and several minerals.

BEEF & NOODLE soup

Serves
6

Preparation
15 min.

Cooking
3¼ hr.

Level
Medium

- 2 pounds (1 kg) beef bones
- 3 quarts (3 liters) cold water
- 2 large onions, chopped
- 1 (2-inch/5-cm) piece ginger, thinly sliced
- 5 star anise
- 2 cinnamon sticks
- 1 teaspoon black peppercorns
- 5 whole cloves
- 1 tablespoon coriander seeds
- 2 tablespoons Thai fish sauce
- 2 tablespoons lime juice + wedges, to serve
  Salt and freshly ground black pepper
- 4 ounces (120 g) thick rice noodles
- 8 ounces (250 g) beef fillet steak, very thinly sliced
- 2 cups (100 g) bean sprouts
- 3 scallions (spring onions), thinly sliced
- 2 red chilies, thinly sliced
- ½ cup fresh mint leaves
- ½ cup fresh cilantro (coriander) leaves

Place the beef bones, water, onions, ginger, star anise, cinnamon, peppercorns, cloves, and coriander seeds in a large soup pot over high heat. Bring to a boil, then decrease the heat to very low and simmer for 3 hours, skimming the surface occasionally with a slotted spoon. The liquid should reduce by half.

Remove from the heat and strain through a fine-mesh sieve into a clean pot. Remove and reserve any meat from the bones and discard the remaining solids.

Place the soup over high heat and bring to a boil. Add the fish sauce and lime juice and stir to combine. Season with salt and pepper.

Meanwhile, place the noodles in a large heatproof bowl and cover with boiling water. Let soak for 5 minutes, or according to the instructions on the package. Drain well.

Divide the noodles evenly among six serving bowls. Top with the sliced beef and any reserved meat from the bones. Ladle the boiling soup into the bowls, and top with bean sprouts, scallions, chilies, mint, and cilantro. Serve hot, with the lime wedges.

This oriental soup is packed with flavor and sustenance. Serve hot as a complete meal in itself. Because the beef is cooked right at the end with the heat of the soup, make sure that it is very thinly sliced and that the soup you ladle over it is boiling hot.

BEEF & PASTA soup

Serves
6

Preparation
30 min.

Cooking
2½ hr.

Level
Easy

2	tablespoons extra-virgin olive oil
1	pound (500 g) beef cheeks, trimmed, and cut into small cubes
	Salt and freshly ground black pepper
2	carrots, finely chopped
2	stalks celery, finely chopped
2	cloves garlic, finely chopped
1	onion, finely chopped
⅓	cup (90 g) tomato paste
½	cup (120 ml) dry red wine
1	(14-ounce/400-g) can chopped tomatoes, with juice
4	cups (1 liter) beef stock (see page 8)
4	ounces (120 g) risoni pasta (orzo)
2	cups (100 g) baby spinach leaves
	Parmesan flakes, to serve
	Pesto, to serve
	Freshly baked bread, to serve

Heat the oil in a large soup pot over medium-high heat. Season the beef with salt and pepper. Add to the pot in batches and sauté until browned all over, 4–5 minutes each batch. Set aside.

Add the carrots, celery, garlic, and onion to the pot and sauté until the vegetables start to soften, about 5 minutes. Return the beef to the pot, along with the tomato paste, and stir for 1 minute. Add the wine, tomatoes, and beef stock and bring to a boil. Decrease the heat to low, partially cover, and simmer until the beef is very tender, about 2 hours.

Add the risoni and cook until al dente. Stir in the spinach and simmer until just wilted, 2–3 minutes.

Ladle the soup into serving bowls and serve hot with Parmesan, pesto, and bread.

This soup really is a meal-in-a-bowl. Serve it hot for dinner, with plenty of fresh bread to mop up the liquid. You can buy fresh basil pesto, or follow the instructions in the note at the bottom of page 30, and make your own at home.

INDEX